S0-DXJ-548

Visit the
STATUE OF
LIBERTY

By Siobhan Moriarty

Gareth Stevens
Publishing

Please visit our website, www.garethstevens.com. For a free color catalog of all our high-quality books, call toll free 1-800-542-2595 or fax 1-877-542-2596.

Library of Congress Cataloging-in-Publication Data

Moriarty, Siobhan.
Visit the Statue of Liberty / Siobhan Moriarty.
    p. cm. — (Landmarks of liberty)
Includes index.
ISBN 978-1-4339-6402-2 (pbk.)
ISBN 978-1-4339-6403-9 (6-pack)
ISBN 978-1-4339-6400-8 (library binding)
1. Statue of Liberty (New York, N.Y.)—Juvenile literature. 2. Statue of Liberty National Monument (N.Y. and N.J.)—Juvenile literature. 3. New York (N.Y.)—Buildings, structures, etc.—Juvenile literature. I. Title.
F128.64.L6M68 2012
974.7'1—dc23

                                        2011033651

First Edition

Published in 2012 by
Gareth Stevens Publishing
111 East 14th Street, Suite 349
New York, NY 10003

Copyright © 2012 Gareth Stevens Publishing

Designer: Andrea Davison-Bartolotta
Editor: Therese Shea

Photo credits: Cover (except main image), back cover (all), (pp. 2–3, 21, 22–23, 24 flag background), (pp. 4–21 corkboard background), pp. 4, 5, 7 (main image), 11, 12 Shutterstock.com; cover (main image), p. 1 Jose Miguel Hernandez/Flickr/Getty Images; pp. 7 (inset), 15 (inset) Wikimedia Commons; pp. 9, 15 (main image) Hulton Archive/Getty Images; p. 13 Musee Bartholdi/Authenticated/Getty Images; p. 17 Michael S. Yamashita/National Geographic/Getty Images; p. 19 Amanda Hall/Robert Harding World Imagery/Getty Images; p. 20 Bernard Gotfryd/Getty Images.

Printed in the United States of America

CPSIA compliance information: Batch #CW12GS: For further information contact Gareth Stevens, New York, New York at 1-800-542-2595.

Contents

Words in the glossary appear in **bold** type the first time they are used in the text.

Lady Liberty

Besides our national flag, no **symbol** of the United States is better known to people around the world than the Statue of **Liberty**. Standing tall on an island in New York Harbor, she welcomes visitors traveling by boat to New York City.

But how did this robed lady become a symbol of liberty? You may be surprised! The story of Lady Liberty, as the Statue of Liberty is sometimes called, begins in France, not the United States.

The Statue of Liberty is made of copper. Over many years, water and air mixed with the surface and gave the statue its green appearance.

Our Friend, France

France has been a friendly nation to the United States for a long time. During the American **Revolution**, France provided money and soldiers to help Americans fight England and gain their freedom. The people of France watched as the United States set up a government controlled by its citizens. They respected its strength, even during terrible moments such as the American Civil War.

Around 1865, a French official named Edouard de Laboulaye had an idea. The two countries could construct a statue together. The statue would stand for friendship and freedom.

The Statue of Liberty holds a tablet in her left hand. On it is the date that Congress approved the Declaration of Independence.

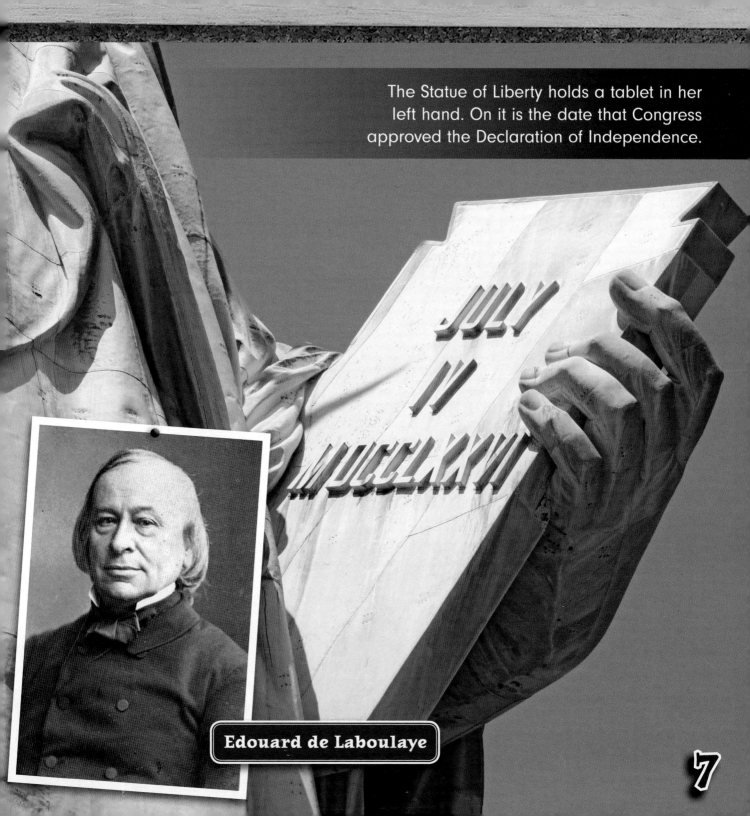

Edouard de Laboulaye

A Perfect Place

Laboulaye chose the famous **sculptor** Frederic-Auguste Bartholdi to create the statue. In 1874, Bartholdi sailed to the United States to find support for the project as well as a location for it.

As Bartholdi sailed into New York Harbor, he saw an island named Bedloe's Island. He thought the location would be perfect. Everyone coming to New York would see the statue on this island. Bartholdi began his **design** when he returned to France.

Tell Me More!

Bartholdi designed the face of the Statue of Liberty to look like his mother's face.

Bartholdi, shown here, wanted his statue for the United States to look like an ancient Greek or Roman statue.

9

The Design

Several years before, Bartholdi had designed a monument in Egypt that had never been built. It was going to be a lighthouse that looked like a woman carrying a **torch**. Bartholdi thought this idea would work well for the American monument as well.

In America, Richard Morris Hunt was chosen to design the pedestal, or base, on which the statue would stand. Hunt, who had studied art in Paris, France, didn't want the pedestal to stand out. He wanted all the attention to be drawn to the statue.

Tell Me More!

The French people donated, or gave, about $400,000 for the building of the statue.

The Statue of Liberty's pedestal is made of concrete, granite, and steel. At the time it was completed, it was the largest concrete structure in the world!

11

Building

Bartholdi asked French **engineer** Alexandre Gustave Eiffel to make a frame for the statue. Eiffel made a strong iron tower. Then he used **flexible** iron bars and steel rods to join the tower to the outside surface of the statue. This way, the statue could sway in strong winds instead of being blown over.

Bartholdi made the statue's "skin." He created the statue's shapes by hammering sheets of copper from the inside. The finished skin was just 3/32 inch (2.4 mm) thick! That's about as thin as two pennies.

Tell Me More!

Eiffel later built the famous Eiffel Tower in Paris, France.

The Statue of Liberty, shown here in pieces in Bartholdi's Paris workshop, was completed in France in July 1884. It was then taken apart and shipped in 214 boxes to the United States.

13

The Dedication

While the French were completing the statue, the Americans were having a hard time collecting enough donations to finish the pedestal. Finally, newspaper publisher Joseph Pulitzer asked for help on the front page of his newspaper. Enough money was collected to complete the pedestal in 1886. The statue was then put together. Electric lights were placed in the torch.

On October 28, 1886, thousands of people, including President Grover Cleveland and Bartholdi, attended the **dedication** of the monument.

Tell Me More!

The official name of the Statue of Liberty is "Statue of Liberty **Enlightening** the World."

In this 1884 drawing, workers pose next to what would become the base of the pedestal for the statue.

painting of the unveiling of the Statue of Liberty

A Welcoming Symbol

The Statue of Liberty, as it came to be called, quickly became a symbol of the United States. While it still stood for the friendship between two nations, it also became a promise of freedom to the millions of **immigrants** who sailed into New York Harbor.

To honor the statue as a welcoming landmark to immigrants, a poem was placed on the pedestal in 1903. Called "The New **Colossus**," this poem by Emma Lazarus describes how Lady Liberty lifts her light to guide immigrants to a new life.

Tell Me More!

The broken chain around the statue's feet stands for the idea that the chains of unjust rule were broken after the American Revolution.

This photo shows the distance between the Statue of Liberty and Ellis Island, where immigrants once had to stop before entering the United States.

Ellis Island

A National Park

At first, the Statue of Liberty was cared for as a lighthouse because of the light glowing from the torch. In 1924, it was officially named a national monument. In 1933, the National Park Service began to care for the statue. Bedloe's Island was renamed Liberty Island in 1956.

Nearby Ellis Island is now a part of the Statue of Liberty National Monument as well. Today, thousands of people visit the Statue of Liberty and Ellis Island each day.

Tell Me More!

National Park Service workers climb a 40-foot (12 m) ladder in order to maintain the statue's torch.

People take a special boat from New York or New Jersey to the Statue of Liberty.

STATUE OF LIBERTY & ELLIS ISLAND

19

Visiting the Statue of Liberty

Anyone can travel to Liberty Island and look at the Statue of Liberty from the ground. However, to enter the monument requires a special ticket. Only about 3,000 people a day can go in the pedestal. Only 240 are permitted to go up to the crown.

Visitors couldn't visit the inside of the statue for nearly 3 years following the **terrorist** attacks of September 11, 2001. The crown was finally reopened to visitors on Independence Day 2009. Lady Liberty remains a beloved symbol of freedom to people around the world.

The Statue of Liberty was restored for its hundredth birthday in 1986.

More About the Statue of Liberty

Height:

151 feet 1 inch (46.05 m), from feet to torch

Fun Fact:

When the Statue of Liberty was first put together in the United States, the head and right arm were attached a couple of feet away from where they were supposed to be. The mistake wasn't fixed until the 1980s!

Number of Steps to the Crown:

354

Number of Lamps in Torch:

16

21

Glossary

colossus: a statue that is several times larger than life size

dedication: an event to mark the official completion of something

design: to create the pattern or shape of something. Also, the pattern or shape of it.

engineer: one who plans or oversees the building of something

enlighten: to give knowledge

flexible: able to bend

immigrant: one who comes to a country to settle there

liberty: freedom

revolution: the overthrow of a government

sculptor: an artist who creates shapes with stone, wood, metal, or other matter

symbol: something that stands for something else

terrorist: someone who uses violence and fear to challenge an authority

torch: a stick of wood that is set on fire and carried as a source of light

For More Information

Books

Behrens, Janice. *What Is the Statue of Liberty?* New York, NY: Children's Press, 2009.

Braithwaite, Jill. *The Statue of Liberty*. Minneapolis, MN: Lerner Publishing, 2011.

Staton, Hilarie. *The Statue of Liberty*. New York, NY: Chelsea Clubhouse, 2010.

Websites

The Statue of Liberty–Ellis Island Foundation
www.statueofliberty.org
Read much more about both the Statue of Liberty and Ellis Island.

Statue of Liberty National Monument
www.nps.gov/stli
Plan your visit to the Statue of Liberty.

Index